*"Don't be ashamed of your story...
it will inspire others."*

Date _____ Day
S M T W T F S

"Every worthy act is difficult. Ascent is always difficult. Descent is easy and often slippery." – Mahatma Gandhi

Today's Affirmation:
_____
_____
_____

Thoughts about today:
_____
_____
_____
_____
_____
_____
_____
_____

My Mood Today

1 2 3 4 5 6 7 8 9 10

I stayed sober today: ◯ YES   ◯ NO

Date _____ Day
S M T W T F S

"Our greatest glory is not in never failing, but in rising up every time we fail." – Ralph Waldo Emerson

Today's Affirmation:
_____
_____
_____
_____

Thoughts about today:
_____
_____
_____
_____
_____
_____
_____
_____

My Mood Today

1   2   3   4   5   6   7   8   9   10

I stayed sober today: ◯ YES   ◯ NO

Date

Day
S M T W T F S

"Sometimes you can only find Heaven by slowly backing away from Hell." – Carrie Fisher

Today's Affirmation:

Thoughts about today:

My Mood Today

1 2 3 4 5 6 7 8 9 10

I stayed sober today: ◯ YES ◯ NO

Date .... Day
S M T W T F S

"The best time to plant a tree was 20 years ago. The second best time is now." – Chinese proverb

Today's Affirmation:

_____
_____
_____

Thoughts about today:

_____
_____
_____
_____
_____
_____
_____
_____

My Mood Today

1 2 3 4 5 6 7 8 9 10

I stayed sober today: ◯ YES   ◯ NO

Date .... Day
S M T W T F S

"As we go through the day we pause, when agitated or doubtful, and ask for the right thought or action." ~ Alcoholics Anonymous

Today's Affirmation:

_____
_____
_____
_____

Thoughts about today:

_____
_____
_____
_____
_____
_____
_____
_____
_____
_____

My Mood Today

1   2   3   4   5   6   7   8   9   10

I stayed sober today: ◯ YES   ◯ NO

Date _____ Day
S M T W T F S

"What gets measured gets managed." ~ Kim Miller

Today's Affirmation:

_____
_____
_____

Thoughts about today:

_____
_____
_____
_____
_____
_____
_____
_____

My Mood Today

1 2 3 4 5 6 7 8 9 10

I stayed sober today: ◯ YES   ◯ NO

Date .... Day
S M T W T F S

My recovery must come first so that everything I love in life doesn't have to come last. – Anonymous

Today's Affirmation:

_____
_____
_____

Thoughts about today:

_____
_____
_____
_____
_____
_____
_____
_____

My Mood Today

1 2 3 4 5 6 7 8 9 10

I stayed sober today: ◯ YES ◯ NO

Date _____ **Day**
S M T W T F S

If you find yourself in a hole, the first thing to do is stop digging.
– Anonymous

Today's Affirmation:

_____
_____
_____
_____

Thoughts about today:

_____
_____
_____
_____
_____
_____
_____
_____

My Mood Today

1   2   3   4   5   6   7   8   9   10

I stayed sober today: ◯ YES   ◯ NO

Date .... Day

S M T W T F S

"People often say that motivation doesn't last. Neither does bathing. That's why we recommend it daily." – Zig Ziglar

Today's Affirmation:

_____
_____
_____

Thoughts about today:

_____
_____
_____
_____
_____
_____
_____
_____

My Mood Today

1 2 3 4 5 6 7 8 9 10

I stayed sober today: ◯ YES ◯ NO

Date _____ **Day**
S M T W T F S

"The opposite of addiction is not sobriety, but human connection." – Johann Hari

Today's Affirmation:
_____
_____
_____
_____

Thoughts about today:
_____
_____
_____
_____
_____
_____
_____
_____

My Mood Today

1   2   3   4   5   6   7   8   9   10

I stayed sober today: ○ YES   ○ NO

Date _____ Day
S M T W T F S

"Sometimes the bad things that happen in our lives put us directly on the path to the best things that will ever happen to us." – Nicole Reed

Today's Affirmation:

Thoughts about today:

My Mood Today

1 2 3 4 5 6 7 8 9 10

I stayed sober today: ◯ YES   ◯ NO

Date _____ Day
S M T W T F S

"The most common way people give up power is by thinking they don't have any." – Alice Walker

Today's Affirmation: _____

_____
_____
_____

Thoughts about today:

_____
_____
_____
_____
_____
_____
_____

My Mood Today

1   2   3   4   5   6   7   8   9   10

I stayed sober today: ◯ YES   ◯ NO

Date _____ **Day**
S M T W T F S

"All the suffering, stress, and addiction comes from not realizing you already are what you are looking for." – Jon Kabat-Zinn

Today's Affirmation:
_____
_____
_____
_____

Thoughts about today:
_____
_____
_____
_____
_____
_____
_____
_____

My Mood Today

1 2 3 4 5 6 7 8 9 10

I stayed sober today: ◯ YES ◯ NO

Date .... Day

S M T W T F S

"Experience is not what happens to you, it is what you do with what happens to you." – Aldous Huxley

Today's Affirmation: _____

_____
_____
_____

Thoughts about today:

_____
_____
_____
_____
_____
_____
_____

My Mood Today

1   2   3   4   5   6   7   8   9   10

I stayed sober today: ◯ YES   ◯ NO

Date .... Day
S M T W T F S

"Success is the sum of small efforts, repeated day in and day out."
– Robert Collier

Today's Affirmation:

Thoughts about today:

My Mood Today

1 2 3 4 5 6 7 8 9 10

I stayed sober today: ◯ YES ◯ NO

Date .... **Day**

S M T W T F S

"If you can quit for a day, you can quit for a lifetime." –
Benjamin Alire Sáenz

Today's Affirmation:

_____
_____
_____

Thoughts about today:

_____
_____
_____
_____
_____
_____
_____
_____

My Mood Today

1   2   3   4   5   6   7   8   9   10

I stayed sober today: ◯ YES   ◯ NO

Date _____ Day
S M T W T F S

"Believe you can and you're halfway there." – Theodore Roosevelt

Today's Affirmation:

_____
_____
_____

Thoughts about today:

_____
_____
_____
_____
_____
_____
_____

My Mood Today

1 2 3 4 5 6 7 8 9 10

I stayed sober today: ◯ YES   ◯ NO

Date _____ **Day**

S M T W T F S

"Nothing is impossible; the word itself says, 'I'm possible!'" — Audrey Hepburn

Today's Affirmation: _____

_____
_____
_____

Thoughts about today: _____

_____
_____
_____
_____
_____
_____
_____

My Mood Today

1   2   3   4   5   6   7   8   9   10

I stayed sober today: ◯ YES   ◯ NO

Date _____   Day
S M T W T F S

"Success is the sum of small efforts, repeated day in and day out."
– Robert Collier

Today's Affirmation: _____
_____
_____
_____

Thoughts about today: _____
_____
_____
_____
_____
_____
_____
_____

My Mood Today

1   2   3   4   5   6   7   8   9   10

I stayed sober today: ◯ YES   ◯ NO

Date _____ **Day**

S M T W T F S

"Sometimes you've just got to give yourself what you wish someone else would give you." – Dr. Phil

Today's Affirmation: _____

_____
_____
_____

Thoughts about today:

_____
_____
_____
_____
_____
_____
_____

My Mood Today

1 2 3 4 5 6 7 8 9 10

I stayed sober today: ◯ YES   ◯ NO

Date _____ Day
S M T W T F S

"Don't let the past steal your present." –Terri Guillemets

Today's Affirmation: _____
_____
_____
_____

Thoughts about today: _____
_____
_____
_____
_____
_____
_____
_____

My Mood Today

1   2   3   4   5   6   7   8   9   10

I stayed sober today: ◯ YES   ◯ NO

Date .... **Day**

S M T W T F S

"I avoid looking forward or backward, and try to keep looking upward." – Charlotte Brontë

Today's Affirmation:

_____
_____
_____

Thoughts about today:

_____
_____
_____
_____
_____
_____
_____

My Mood Today

1 2 3 4 5 6 7 8 9 10

I stayed sober today: ◯ YES   ◯ NO

Date _____ Day
S M T W T F S

"You must do the things you think you cannot do."
– Eleanor Roosevelt

Today's Affirmation:
_____
_____
_____
_____

Thoughts about today:
_____
_____
_____
_____
_____
_____
_____
_____

My Mood Today

1   2   3   4   5   6   7   8   9   10

I stayed sober today: ◯ YES   ◯ NO

Date _____ Day
S M T W T F S

"I can't change the direction of the wind, but I can adjust my sails to always reach my destination." – Jimmy Dean

Today's Affirmation: _____
_____
_____
_____

Thoughts about today:
_____
_____
_____
_____
_____
_____
_____
_____

My Mood Today

1 2 3 4 5 6 7 8 9 10

I stayed sober today: ◯ YES   ◯ NO

Date _____ **Day**
S M T W T F S

"What makes the desert beautiful is that somewhere it hides a well."
– Antoine de Saint-Exupery

Today's Affirmation:
_____
_____
_____
_____

Thoughts about today:
_____
_____
_____
_____
_____
_____
_____
_____
_____

My Mood Today

1   2   3   4   5   6   7   8   9   10

I stayed sober today: ◯ YES   ◯ NO

Date .... Day
S M T W T F S

"The only journey is the one within." – Rainer Maria Rilke

Today's Affirmation: _____

_____
_____
_____
_____

Thoughts about today: _____

_____
_____
_____
_____
_____
_____
_____
_____

My Mood Today

1   2   3   4   5   6   7   8   9   10

I stayed sober today: ◯ YES   ◯ NO

Date ....

Day
S M T W T F S

"Never say anything about yourself you do not want to come true." – Brian Tracy

Today's Affirmation:

Thoughts about today:

My Mood Today

1 2 3 4 5 6 7 8 9 10

I stayed sober today: ◯ YES ◯ NO

Date .... Day
S M T W T F S

"As one goes through life, one learns that if you don't paddle your own canoe, you don't move." – Katharine Hepburn

Today's Affirmation:
_____
_____
_____
_____

Thoughts about today:
_____
_____
_____
_____
_____
_____
_____
_____

My Mood Today

1   2   3   4   5   6   7   8   9   10

I stayed sober today: ◯ YES   ◯ NO

Date .... Day

S M T W T F S

"If you don't know where you are going, you'll end up someplace else." – Yogi Berra

Today's Affirmation:

Thoughts about today:

My Mood Today

1 2 3 4 5 6 7 8 9 10

I stayed sober today: ◯ YES   ◯ NO

Date .... Day
S M T W T F S

"The best way out is always through." – Robert Frost

Today's Affirmation:
_____
_____
_____
_____

Thoughts about today:
_____
_____
_____
_____
_____
_____
_____
_____

My Mood Today

1 2 3 4 5 6 7 8 9 10

I stayed sober today: ◯ YES   ◯ NO

Date .... Day
S M T W T F S

"Experience is not what happens to you, it is what you do with what happens to you." – Aldous Huxley

Today's Affirmation:

_____
_____
_____
_____

Thoughts about today:

_____
_____
_____
_____
_____
_____
_____
_____

My Mood Today

1   2   3   4   5   6   7   8   9   10

I stayed sober today: ◯ YES   ◯ NO

Date .... Day

S M T W T F S

Today is the bridge between acceptance and faith.
- Jonathan Lockwood Huie

Today's Affirmation:

_____
_____
_____
_____

Thoughts about today:

_____
_____
_____
_____
_____
_____
_____
_____

My Mood Today

1   2   3   4   5   6   7   8   9   10

I stayed sober today: ○ YES   ○ NO

Date _____ **Day**
S M T W T F S

"Keep steadily before you the fact that all true success depends at last upon yourself." – Theodore T. Hunger

Today's Affirmation:
_____
_____
_____
_____

Thoughts about today:
_____
_____
_____
_____
_____
_____
_____
_____

My Mood Today

1   2   3   4   5   6   7   8   9   10

I stayed sober today: ○ YES ○ NO

Date .... **Day**
S M T W T F S

"Every noble work is at first impossible." – Thomas Carlyle

Today's Affirmation: _____
_____
_____
_____

Thoughts about today: _____
_____
_____
_____
_____
_____
_____
_____

My Mood Today

1 2 3 4 5 6 7 8 9 10

I stayed sober today: ○ YES   ○ NO

Date .... Day
S M T W T F S

Fall seven times, stand up eight." – Japanese proverb

Today's Affirmation:
_____
_____
_____
_____

Thoughts about today:
_____
_____
_____
_____
_____
_____
_____
_____
_____

My Mood Today

1 2 3 4 5 6 7 8 9 10

I stayed sober today: ◯ YES ◯ NO

Date _____ **Day** S M T W T F S

"Turn your face to the sun and the shadows fall behind you."
– Charlotte Whitton

Today's Affirmation: _____
_____
_____
_____

Thoughts about today: _____
_____
_____
_____
_____
_____
_____
_____
_____

My Mood Today

1   2   3   4   5   6   7   8   9   10

I stayed sober today: ◯ YES   ◯ NO

Date _____ Day
S M T W T F S

"Not feeling is no replacement for reality. Your problems today are still your problems tomorrow." – Larry Michael Dredla

Today's Affirmation: _____
_____
_____
_____

Thoughts about today: _____
_____
_____
_____
_____
_____
_____
_____

My Mood Today

1   2   3   4   5   6   7   8   9   10

I stayed sober today: ◯ YES   ◯ NO

Date: _____ Day:
S M T W T F S

The most common way people give up their power is by thinking they don't have any." – Alice Walker

Today's Affirmation:
_____
_____
_____
_____

Thoughts about today:
_____
_____
_____
_____
_____
_____
_____
_____

My Mood Today

1   2   3   4   5   6   7   8   9   10

I stayed sober today: ◯ YES   ◯ NO

Date _____ Day

S M T W T F S

"Life is like riding a bicycle. To keep your balance you must keep moving." – Albert Einstein

Today's Affirmation:

Thoughts about today:

My Mood Today

1 2 3 4 5 6 7 8 9 10

I stayed sober today: ◯ YES ◯ NO

Date _____ Day
S M T W T F S

"Patience and the mulberry leaf becomes a silk gown."
– Chinese proverb

Today's Affirmation: _____

_____
_____
_____

Thoughts about today: _____

_____
_____
_____
_____
_____
_____
_____

My Mood Today

1   2   3   4   5   6   7   8   9   10

I stayed sober today: ◯ YES   ◯ NO

Date .... Day
S M T W T F S

"It always seems impossible until it's done." – Nelson Mandela

Today's Affirmation:
_____
_____
_____
_____

Thoughts about today:
_____
_____
_____
_____
_____
_____
_____
_____

My Mood Today

1 2 3 4 5 6 7 8 9 10

I stayed sober today: ○ YES   ○ NO

Date

Day
S M T W T F S

"If things go wrong, don't go with them." – Roger Babson

Today's Affirmation:

Thoughts about today:

My Mood Today

1 2 3 4 5 6 7 8 9 10

I stayed sober today: ○ YES ○ NO

Date ....

Day
S M T W T F S

"Every strike brings me closer to the next home run."
— *Babe Ruth*

Today's Affirmation:

Thoughts about today:

My Mood Today

1 2 3 4 5 6 7 8 9 10

I stayed sober today: ◯ YES   ◯ NO

Date .... **Day**
S M T W T F S

"Rock bottom became the solid foundation on which I rebuilt myself." ~Unknown

Today's Affirmation:

Thoughts about today:

My Mood Today

1   2   3   4   5   6   7   8   9   10

I stayed sober today: ○ YES ○ NO

Date .... Day
S M T W T F S

"It is not I who became addicted. It is my body." — Jean Cocteau

Today's Affirmation:

_____
_____
_____
_____

Thoughts about today:

_____
_____
_____
_____
_____
_____
_____
_____
_____

My Mood Today

1 2 3 4 5 6 7 8 9 10

I stayed sober today: ◯ YES ◯ NO

Date _____ Day
S M T W T F S

"One step at a time. One day at a time. One hour at a time." — Unknown

Today's Affirmation: _____
_____
_____
_____

Thoughts about today: _____
_____
_____
_____
_____
_____
_____
_____
_____

My Mood Today

1 2 3 4 5 6 7 8 9 10

I stayed sober today: ◯ YES   ◯ NO

Date _____ Day
S M T W T F S

"It was the hardest boyfriend I ever had to break up with." ~Fergie

Today's Affirmation:
_____
_____
_____
_____

Thoughts about today:
_____
_____
_____
_____
_____
_____
_____

My Mood Today

1 2 3 4 5 6 7 8 9 10

I stayed sober today: ○ YES   ○ NO

Date .... Day
S M T W T F S

"Remember just because you hit bottom doesn't mean you have to stay there." — Robert Downey Jr.

Today's Affirmation: _____

_____
_____
_____

Thoughts about today: _____

_____
_____
_____
_____
_____
_____
_____

My Mood Today

1   2   3   4   5   6   7   8   9   10

I stayed sober today: ◯ YES   ◯ NO

Date _____ Day
S M T W T F S

"There's not a drug on earth that can make life meaningful." — Unknown

Today's Affirmation:

_____
_____
_____
_____

Thoughts about today:

_____
_____
_____
_____
_____
_____
_____
_____

My Mood Today

1 2 3 4 5 6 7 8 9 10

I stayed sober today: ◯ YES ◯ NO

Date: _____ Day

S M T W T F S

"Recovery is not for people who need it. It's for people who want it." — Unknown

Today's Affirmation: _____

_____
_____
_____

Thoughts about today: _____

_____
_____
_____
_____
_____
_____
_____

My Mood Today

1   2   3   4   5   6   7   8   9   10

I stayed sober today: ○ YES   ○ NO

Date ....

Day
S M T W T F S

"If you chased your recovery like you chased your high, you would never relapse again." — Unknown

Today's Affirmation:

_____
_____
_____
_____

Thoughts about today:

_____
_____
_____
_____
_____
_____
_____
_____

My Mood Today

1   2   3   4   5   6   7   8   9   10

I stayed sober today: ◯ YES ◯ NO

Date _____ Day
S M T W T F S

"It's a beautiful day to be sober." — Unknown

Today's Affirmation: _____
_____
_____
_____

Thoughts about today: _____
_____
_____
_____
_____
_____
_____
_____

My Mood Today

1   2   3   4   5   6   7   8   9   10

I stayed sober today: ○ YES   ○ NO

Date _____

Day
S M T W T F S

"Hardships often prepare ordinary people for an extraordinary destiny." — C.S. Lewis

Today's Affirmation:
_____
_____
_____
_____

Thoughts about today:
_____
_____
_____
_____
_____
_____
_____
_____

My Mood Today

1 2 3 4 5 6 7 8 9 10

I stayed sober today: ◯ YES   ◯ NO

Date .... **Day**

S M T W T F S

"Recovery is about progression, not perfection." — Unknown

Today's Affirmation: _____

_____
_____
_____

Thoughts about today: _____

_____
_____
_____
_____
_____
_____
_____

My Mood Today

1   2   3   4   5   6   7   8   9   10

I stayed sober today: ◯ YES   ◯ NO

Date .... # Day
S M T W T F S

*"It does not matter how slowly you go,
as long as you do not stop."* — Confucius

Today's Affirmation:

Thoughts about today:

My Mood Today

1   2   3   4   5   6   7   8   9   10

I stayed sober today: ◯ YES   ◯ NO

Date .... **Day**
S M T W T F S

"It is often in the darkest skies that we see the brightest stars." — Richard Evans

Today's Affirmation:

_____

_____

_____

_____

Thoughts about today:

_____

_____

_____

_____

_____

_____

_____

_____

My Mood Today

1 2 3 4 5 6 7 8 9 10

I stayed sober today: ◯ YES   ◯ NO

Date _____   Day
S   M   T   W   T   F   S

*"I used drugs to feel better.
I quit drugs to be better."* — Unknown

Today's Affirmation:
_____
_____
_____
_____

Thoughts about today:
_____
_____
_____
_____
_____
_____
_____
_____

My Mood Today

1   2   3   4   5   6   7   8   9   10

I stayed sober today: ◯ YES   ◯ NO

Date _____ **Day**
S M T W T F S

"No matter how dark the moment, love and hope are always possible." — George Chakiris

Today's Affirmation: _____
_____
_____
_____

Thoughts about today: _____
_____
_____
_____
_____
_____
_____
_____

My Mood Today

1   2   3   4   5   6   7   8   9   10

I stayed sober today: ◯ YES   ◯ NO

Date: _____ Day: S M T W T F S

"That which does not kill us makes us stronger."
Friedrich Nietzsche

Today's Affirmation:
_____
_____
_____
_____

Thoughts about today:
_____
_____
_____
_____
_____
_____
_____
_____

My Mood Today

1 2 3 4 5 6 7 8 9 10

I stayed sober today: ◯ YES   ◯ NO

Date .... **Day**

S M T W T F S

"The world breaks everyone and afterward many are strong at the broken places." ~ Ernest Hemingway

Today's Affirmation:

_____
_____
_____
_____

Thoughts about today:

_____
_____
_____
_____
_____
_____
_____
_____

My Mood Today

1   2   3   4   5   6   7   8   9   10

I stayed sober today: ◯ YES   ◯ NO

Date .... **Day**
S M T W T F S

"You know you're an alcoholic when you misplace things ... like a decade." — Paul Williams

Today's Affirmation:

_____
_____
_____

Thoughts about today:

_____
_____
_____
_____
_____
_____
_____

My Mood Today

1   2   3   4   5   6   7   8   9   10

I stayed sober today: ◯ YES   ◯ NO

Date _____   **Day**
S M T W T F S

"If you know someone who tries to drown their sorrows, you might tell them that sorrows know how to swim." — Ann Landers

Today's Affirmation: _____
_____
_____
_____

Thoughts about today: _____
_____
_____
_____
_____
_____
_____
_____

My Mood Today

1   2   3   4   5   6   7   8   9   10

I stayed sober today: ◯ YES   ◯ NO

Date _____ **Day**
S M T W T F S

"I have not failed. I've just found 10,000 ways that won't work." — Thomas Edison

Today's Affirmation: _____

_____

_____

_____

Thoughts about today: _____

_____

_____

_____

_____

_____

_____

_____

My Mood Today

1   2   3   4   5   6   7   8   9   10

I stayed sober today: ◯ YES   ◯ NO

Date .... Day
S M T W T F S

"Life is like riding a bicycle. To keep your balance you must keep moving." – Albert Einstein

Today's Affirmation: _____
_____
_____
_____

Thoughts about today: _____
_____
_____
_____
_____
_____
_____
_____
_____
_____

My Mood Today

1   2   3   4   5   6   7   8   9   10

I stayed sober today: ◯ YES   ◯ NO

Date _____ Day

S M T W T F S

"A problem is a chance for you to do your best." ~Duke Ellington

Today's Affirmation:

_____
_____
_____
_____

Thoughts about today:

_____
_____
_____
_____
_____
_____
_____
_____

My Mood Today

1   2   3   4   5   6   7   8   9   10

I stayed sober today: ◯ YES   ◯ NO

Date _____ Day

S M T W T F S

"When you have faith, everything is possible. "~Unknown

Today's Affirmation:

_____
_____
_____
_____

Thoughts about today:

_____
_____
_____
_____
_____
_____
_____

My Mood Today

1 2 3 4 5 6 7 8 9 10

I stayed sober today: ◯ YES   ◯ NO

Date ....

Day
S M T W T F S

"You only live one but if you do it right, once is enough." — Mae West

Today's Affirmation:

_____
_____
_____

Thoughts about today:

_____
_____
_____
_____
_____
_____
_____

My Mood Today

1   2   3   4   5   6   7   8   9   10

I stayed sober today: ◯ YES   ◯ NO

Date: _____ Day: S M T W T F S

"The mind is everything. What you think, you become." ~Buddha

Today's Affirmation:

Thoughts about today:

My Mood Today

1 2 3 4 5 6 7 8 9 10

I stayed sober today: ○ YES ○ NO

Date _____ **Day** S M T W T F S

"It is important that we forgive ourselves for making mistakes. We need to learn from our errors and move on." — Steve Maraboli

Today's Affirmation:

___

Thoughts about today:

___

My Mood Today

1   2   3   4   5   6   7   8   9   10

I stayed sober today: ◯ YES   ◯ NO

Date .... **Day**
S M T W T F S

"Your willingness to look at your darkness is what empowers you to change." — Iyanla Vanzant

Today's Affirmation:

Thoughts about today:

My Mood Today

1 2 3 4 5 6 7 8 9 10

I stayed sober today: ◯ YES ◯ NO

Date _____ Day
S M T W T F S

"Mistakes are proof that you are trying." ~Unknown

Today's Affirmation:

_____
_____
_____

Thoughts about today:

_____
_____
_____
_____
_____
_____
_____

My Mood Today

1 2 3 4 5 6 7 8 9 10

I stayed sober today: ◯ YES ◯ NO

Date _____ **Day**
S M T W T F S

"If you aren't in over your head, how do you know how tall you are?" -T.S. Eliot

Today's Affirmation: _____

Thoughts about today:

My Mood Today

1 2 3 4 5 6 7 8 9 10

I stayed sober today: ○ YES ○ NO

Date _____ Day
S M T W T F S

"Sometimes by losing a battle you find a new way to win the war." ~Donald Trump

Today's Affirmation: _____
_____
_____
_____

Thoughts about today:
_____
_____
_____
_____
_____
_____
_____

My Mood Today

1   2   3   4   5   6   7   8   9   10

I stayed sober today: ◯ YES   ◯ NO

Date _____ Day
S M T W T F S

"Accept responsibility for your life. Know that it is you who will get you where you want to go, no one else." ~Les Brown

Today's Affirmation:

_____
_____
_____
_____

Thoughts about today:

_____
_____
_____
_____
_____
_____
_____
_____

My Mood Today

1   2   3   4   5   6   7   8   9   10

I stayed sober today: ◯ YES   ◯ NO

Date .... **Day**

S M T W T F S

"We can't plan life. All we can do is be available for it."
~Lauryn Hill

Today's Affirmation:

_____
_____
_____
_____

Thoughts about today:

_____
_____
_____
_____
_____
_____
_____

My Mood Today

1   2   3   4   5   6   7   8   9   10

I stayed sober today: ◯ YES   ◯ NO

Date _____ Day
S M T W T F S

"Strength and growth come only through continuous effort and struggle." ~Napoleon Hill

Today's Affirmation:

_____
_____
_____
_____

Thoughts about today:

_____
_____
_____
_____
_____
_____
_____
_____

My Mood Today

1 2 3 4 5 6 7 8 9 10

I stayed sober today: ◯ YES ◯ NO

Date .... Day
S M T W T F S

"If you want to see a rainbow you have to learn to see the rain."
~Paulo Coelho

Today's Affirmation:

_____
_____
_____
_____

Thoughts about today:

_____
_____
_____
_____
_____
_____
_____

My Mood Today

1   2   3   4   5   6   7   8   9   10

I stayed sober today: ◯ YES   ◯ NO

Date .... **Day**
S M T W T F S

*"The pine stays green in winter...
wisdom in hardship." ~ Norman Douglas*

Today's Affirmation:

_____
_____
_____
_____

Thoughts about today:

_____
_____
_____
_____
_____
_____
_____
_____

My Mood Today

1   2   3   4   5   6   7   8   9   10

I stayed sober today: ◯ YES   ◯ NO

Date _____ Day
S M T W T F S

"Every Flower Is A Soul Blossoming In Nature."
– Gerard de Nerval

Today's Affirmation:

_____
_____
_____
_____

Thoughts about today:

_____
_____
_____
_____
_____
_____
_____
_____

My Mood Today

1   2   3   4   5   6   7   8   9   10

I stayed sober today: ◯ YES   ◯ NO

Date: _____ Day S M T W T F S

"I am no longer accepting the things I can not change. I am changing the things I can not accept" – Dr. Angela Davis

Today's Affirmation:
_____
_____
_____
_____

Thoughts about today:
_____
_____
_____
_____
_____
_____
_____
_____
_____

My Mood Today

1   2   3   4   5   6   7   8   9   10

I stayed sober today: ◯ YES   ◯ NO

Date .... Day
S M T W T F S

"Every man is guilty of all the good he did not do." -Voltaire

Today's Affirmation:

_____
_____
_____

Thoughts about today:

_____
_____
_____
_____
_____
_____
_____

My Mood Today

1   2   3   4   5   6   7   8   9   10

I stayed sober today: ◯ YES   ◯ NO

Date _____ Day
S M T W T F S

"A nail is driven out by another nail. Habit is overcome by habit. -Desiderius Erasmus"

Today's Affirmation:

_____
_____
_____
_____

Thoughts about today:

_____
_____
_____
_____
_____
_____
_____

My Mood Today

1 2 3 4 5 6 7 8 9 10

I stayed sober today: ◯ YES ◯ NO

Date _____ Day
S M T W T F S

"Begin now to be what you will be hereafter." ~Saint Jerome

Today's Affirmation:

_____
_____
_____
_____

Thoughts about today:

_____
_____
_____
_____
_____
_____
_____
_____

My Mood Today

1 2 3 4 5 6 7 8 9 10

I stayed sober today: ◯ YES   ◯ NO

Date .... **Day**　S M T W T F S

"We have to do the best we are capable of. This is our sacred human responsibility." ~Albert Einstein

Today's Affirmation:

Thoughts about today:

My Mood Today

1　2　3　4　5　6　7　8　9　10

I stayed sober today: ◯ YES　◯ NO

Date .... Day
S M T W T F S

"Magic is believing in yourself, if you can do that, you can make anything happen." ~Johann Wolfgang von Goethe

Today's Affirmation:

_____
_____
_____

Thoughts about today:

_____
_____
_____
_____
_____
_____

My Mood Today

1 2 3 4 5 6 7 8 9 10

I stayed sober today: ◯ YES ◯ NO

Date _____ Day
S M T W T F S

"The world is full of magic things, patiently waiting for our senses to grow sharper." ~W.B. Yeats

Today's Affirmation:

_____
_____
_____
_____

Thoughts about today:

_____
_____
_____
_____
_____
_____
_____
_____

My Mood Today

1   2   3   4   5   6   7   8   9   10

I stayed sober today: ◯ YES   ◯ NO

Date ....

Day
S M T W T F S

"We know what we are, but know not what we may be."
~William Shakespeare

Today's Affirmation:
_____
_____
_____
_____

Thoughts about today:
_____
_____
_____
_____
_____
_____
_____
_____

My Mood Today

1   2   3   4   5   6   7   8   9   10

I stayed sober today: ○ YES   ○ NO

Date _____ **Day**
S M T W T F S

"We did not come to fear the future. We came here to shape it."
~Barack Obama

Today's Affirmation:

Thoughts about today:

My Mood Today

1 2 3 4 5 6 7 8 9 10

I stayed sober today: ◯ YES   ◯ NO

Date _____ **Day**
S M T W T F S

"Although the world is full of suffering, it is also full of the overcoming of it." ~Helen Keller

Today's Affirmation:
_____
_____
_____
_____

Thoughts about today:
_____
_____
_____
_____
_____
_____
_____
_____

My Mood Today

1 2 3 4 5 6 7 8 9 10

I stayed sober today: ⚪ YES ⚪ NO

Date _____ Day

S M T W T F S

"Ask and it will be given to you; seek and you will find; knock and the door will be opened to you." ~Jesus Christ

Today's Affirmation: _____
_____
_____
_____

Thoughts about today: _____
_____
_____
_____
_____
_____
_____
_____

My Mood Today

1 2 3 4 5 6 7 8 9 10

I stayed sober today: ○ YES   ○ NO

Date

Day
S M T W T F S

"When you know what you want, and want it bad enough, you will find a way to get it." ~Jim Rohn

Today's Affirmation:

Thoughts about today:

My Mood Today

1 2 3 4 5 6 7 8 9 10

I stayed sober today: ◯ YES ◯ NO

Date _____ Day

S M T W T F S

"Little by little, one travels far." ~ J. R. R. Tolkien

Today's Affirmation: _____

_____
_____
_____

Thoughts about today: _____

_____
_____
_____
_____
_____
_____
_____

My Mood Today

1 2 3 4 5 6 7 8 9 10

I stayed sober today: ◯ YES   ◯ NO

Date .... **Day**
S M T W T F S

""If you don't like something, change it. If you can't change it, change your attitude." ~ Maya Angelou

Today's Affirmation:

Thoughts about today:

My Mood Today

1 2 3 4 5 6 7 8 9 10

I stayed sober today: ◯ YES ◯ NO

Date _____ Day
S M T W T F S

"In three words I can sum up everything I've learned about life: it goes on." ~Robert Frost

Today's Affirmation:
_____
_____
_____
_____

Thoughts about today:
_____
_____
_____
_____
_____
_____
_____
_____

My Mood Today

1 2 3 4 5 6 7 8 9 10

I stayed sober today: ◯ YES ◯ NO

Date _____ Day
S M T W T F S

"Life isn't about finding yourself. Life is about creating yourself."
~George Bernard Shaw

Today's Affirmation:

_____
_____
_____
_____

Thoughts about today:

_____
_____
_____
_____
_____
_____
_____
_____

My Mood Today

1 2 3 4 5 6 7 8 9 10

I stayed sober today: ◯ YES   ◯ NO

Date _____ Day
S M T W T F S

"Your big opportunity may be right where you are now."
~Napoleon Hill

Today's Affirmation: _____
_____
_____
_____

Thoughts about today: _____
_____
_____
_____
_____
_____
_____

My Mood Today

1   2   3   4   5   6   7   8   9   10

I stayed sober today: ◯ YES   ◯ NO

Date .... Day
S M T W T F S

"An ounce of action is worth a ton of theory."~ Friedrich Engels

Today's Affirmation:

_____
_____
_____

Thoughts about today:

_____
_____
_____
_____
_____
_____
_____
_____

My Mood Today

1   2   3   4   5   6   7   8   9   10

I stayed sober today: ◯ YES   ◯ NO

Date _____ **Day**
S M T W T F S

"Paths are made by walking." ~Franz Kafka

Today's Affirmation: _____
_____
_____
_____

Thoughts about today: _____
_____
_____
_____
_____
_____
_____

My Mood Today

1   2   3   4   5   6   7   8   9   10

I stayed sober today: ◯ YES   ◯ NO

Date .... Day
S M T W T F S

"Your mind is a powerful thing. When you fill it with positive thoughts, your life will start to change." ~Unknown

Today's Affirmation:
_____
_____
_____
_____

Thoughts about today:
_____
_____
_____
_____
_____
_____
_____
_____

My Mood Today

1   2   3   4   5   6   7   8   9   10

I stayed sober today: ○ YES   ○ NO

Date .... Day
S M T W T F S

"Breathe, it's just a bad day, not a bad life." ~Unknown

Today's Affirmation:

_____
_____
_____

Thoughts about today:

_____
_____
_____
_____
_____
_____
_____

My Mood Today

1   2   3   4   5   6   7   8   9   10

I stayed sober today: ⚪ YES   ⚪ NO

Date _____ **Day**
S M T W T F S

"I believe that man will not merely endure; he will prevail."
~William Faulkner

Today's Affirmation: _____

_____
_____
_____

Thoughts about today: _____

_____
_____
_____
_____
_____
_____
_____

My Mood Today

1   2   3   4   5   6   7   8   9   10

I stayed sober today: ◯ YES   ◯ NO

Date _____ Day
S M T W T F S

"Embrace the glorious mess that you are." ~Elizabeth Gilbert

Today's Affirmation:
_____
_____
_____
_____

Thoughts about today:
_____
_____
_____
_____
_____
_____
_____
_____

My Mood Today

1   2   3   4   5   6   7   8   9   10

I stayed sober today: ◯ YES   ◯ NO

Date _____   Day
S M T W T F S

"I focused so hard on what I wanted that I lost sight of what I deserved." ~Unknown

Today's Affirmation: _____
_____
_____
_____

Thoughts about today: _____
_____
_____
_____
_____
_____
_____
_____

My Mood Today

1   2   3   4   5   6   7   8   9   10

I stayed sober today: ◯ YES   ◯ NO

Date .... **Day**

S M T W T F S

"We are all in the gutter, but some of us are looking at the stars." ~ Oscar Wilde

Today's Affirmation:

___

Thoughts about today:

___

My Mood Today

1   2   3   4   5   6   7   8   9   10

I stayed sober today: ○ YES   ○ NO

Date .... Day
S M T W T F S

"Some day you will be old enough to start reading fairy tales again." ~C.S. Lewis

Today's Affirmation:

_____
_____
_____
_____

Thoughts about today:

_____
_____
_____
_____
_____
_____
_____

My Mood Today

1 2 3 4 5 6 7 8 9 10

I stayed sober today: ○ YES ○ NO

Date .... Day

S M T W T F S

"Do not ask for what you will wish you had not got.:~Lucius Annaeus Seneca

Today's Affirmation:

_____

_____
_____
_____

Thoughts about today:

_____
_____
_____
_____
_____
_____
_____
_____

My Mood Today

1 2 3 4 5 6 7 8 9 10

I stayed sober today: ◯ YES ◯ NO

Date .... Day
S M T W T F S

"You have to die a few times before you can really live."
~ Charles Bukowski

Today's Affirmation:

_____
_____
_____
_____

Thoughts about today:

_____
_____
_____
_____
_____
_____
_____
_____

My Mood Today

1 2 3 4 5 6 7 8 9 10

I stayed sober today: ◯ YES ◯ NO

Date _____ **Day**
S M T W T F S

"If you suddenly stumble upon the right door, you will not be able to recognize that it is right." ~Osho

Today's Affirmation: _____

_____
_____
_____

Thoughts about today: _____

_____
_____
_____
_____
_____
_____
_____

My Mood Today

1   2   3   4   5   6   7   8   9   10

I stayed sober today: ◯ YES   ◯ NO

Date ....

Day
S M T W T F S

"People cry, not because they're weak. It's because they've been strong for too long." ~Johnny Depp

Today's Affirmation:
_____
_____
_____
_____

Thoughts about today:
_____
_____
_____
_____
_____
_____
_____

My Mood Today
1 2 3 4 5 6 7 8 9 10

I stayed sober today: ○ YES   ○ NO

Date _____ **Day**
S M T W T F S

"Don't look back unless you're planning to go that way." ~Unknown

Today's Affirmation: _____
_____
_____
_____
_____

Thoughts about today:
_____
_____
_____
_____
_____
_____
_____
_____
_____

My Mood Today

1 2 3 4 5 6 7 8 9 10

I stayed sober today: ◯ YES ◯ NO

Date .... **Day**
S M T W T F S

"The most important things are the hardest to say, because words diminish them." ~Stephen King

Today's Affirmation:

_____
_____
_____

Thoughts about today:

_____
_____
_____
_____
_____
_____
_____

My Mood Today

1 2 3 4 5 6 7 8 9 10

I stayed sober today: ◯ YES ◯ NO

Date _____ **Day**
S M T W T F S

"A man who fears suffering is already suffering from what he fears." ~Michel de Montaigne

Today's Affirmation: _____
_____
_____
_____

Thoughts about today:
_____
_____
_____
_____
_____
_____
_____

My Mood Today

1 2 3 4 5 6 7 8 9 10

I stayed sober today: ◯ YES ◯ NO

Date _____ Day
S M T W T F S

"The world breaks everyone, and afterward, some are strong at the broken places." ~Ernest Hemingway

Today's Affirmation: _____
_____
_____
_____

Thoughts about today: _____
_____
_____
_____
_____
_____
_____
_____

My Mood Today

1 2 3 4 5 6 7 8 9 10

I stayed sober today: ○ YES   ○ NO

Date

Day
S M T W T F S

"Be strong enough to stand alone, smart enough to know when you need help, and brave enough to ask for it." ~Unknown

Today's Affirmation:

Thoughts about today:

My Mood Today

1 2 3 4 5 6 7 8 9 10

I stayed sober today: ◯ YES ◯ NO

Date _____ Day
S M T W T F S

"We mature with damage, not with the years." ~Unknown

Today's Affirmation:
_____
_____
_____
_____

Thoughts about today:
_____
_____
_____
_____
_____
_____
_____
_____

My Mood Today

1   2   3   4   5   6   7   8   9   10

I stayed sober today: ○ YES ○ NO

Date: _____ Day
S M T W T F S

"Experience is simply the name we give our mistakes."
~Oscar Wilde

Today's Affirmation: _____
_____
_____
_____
_____

Thoughts about today: _____
_____
_____
_____
_____
_____
_____
_____

My Mood Today

1   2   3   4   5   6   7   8   9   10

I stayed sober today: ◯ YES   ◯ NO

Date ....

Day
S M T W T F S

*"Keep your face always toward the sunshine –
and shadows will fall behind you." ~Walt Whitman*

Today's Affirmation:

_____
_____
_____
_____

Thoughts about today:

_____
_____
_____
_____
_____
_____
_____
_____

My Mood Today

1 2 3 4 5 6 7 8 9 10

I stayed sober today: ◯ YES   ◯ NO

Date

Day
S M T W T F S

"If you fell down yesterday, stand up today." ~ H. G. Wells

Today's Affirmation:

Thoughts about today:

My Mood Today

1 2 3 4 5 6 7 8 9 10

I stayed sober today: ◯ YES ◯ NO

Date _____

Day
S M T W T F S

"Without rain nothing grows. Learn to embrace the storms of your life." ~Unknown

Today's Affirmation: _____
_____
_____
_____

Thoughts about today: _____
_____
_____
_____
_____
_____
_____
_____

My Mood Today

1 2 3 4 5 6 7 8 9 10

I stayed sober today: ◯ YES   ◯ NO

Date _____   **Day**
S M T W T F S

"Stand up to your obstacles and do something about them. You will find that they haven't half the strength you think they have."
~Norman Vincent Peale

Today's Affirmation: _____
_____
_____
_____
_____

Thoughts about today:
_____
_____
_____
_____
_____
_____
_____
_____
_____

My Mood Today

1   2   3   4   5   6   7   8   9   10

I stayed sober today: ○ YES   ○ NO

Date .... **Day**

S M T W T F S

"I survived because the fire inside me burned brighter than the fire around me." ~Unknown

Today's Affirmation:

_____
_____
_____
_____

Thoughts about today:

_____
_____
_____
_____
_____
_____
_____
_____

My Mood Today

1   2   3   4   5   6   7   8   9   10

I stayed sober today: ◯ YES   ◯ NO

Date

Day
S M T W T F S

"Always go with the choice that scares you the most, because that's the one that is going to help you grow." ~Unknown

Today's Affirmation:

Thoughts about today:

My Mood Today

1 2 3 4 5 6 7 8 9 10

I stayed sober today: ◯ YES   ◯ NO

Date _____ **Day**
S M T W T F S

"Let's shake up some shit. That's all you can do."
~Billie Joe Armstrong

Today's Affirmation: _____
_____
_____
_____

Thoughts about today: _____
_____
_____
_____
_____
_____
_____
_____

My Mood Today

1   2   3   4   5   6   7   8   9   10

I stayed sober today: ◯ YES   ◯ NO

Date _____ Day
S M T W T F S

"The art of progress is to preserve order amid change and to preserve change amid order." ~Alfred North Whitehead

Today's Affirmation:

_____
_____
_____
_____

Thoughts about today:

_____
_____
_____
_____
_____
_____
_____
_____

My Mood Today

1   2   3   4   5   6   7   8   9   10

I stayed sober today: ◯ YES   ◯ NO

Date ....

Day
S M T W T F S

"Life is a process. We are a process. The universe is a process."
~ Anne Wilson Scaef

Today's Affirmation:

_____
_____
_____
_____

Thoughts about today:

_____
_____
_____
_____
_____
_____
_____

My Mood Today

1 2 3 4 5 6 7 8 9 10

I stayed sober today: ○ YES   ○ NO

Date ....

Day

S M T W T F S

*"To change one's life, start immediately,
do it flamboyantly, no exceptions." ~ William James*

Today's Affirmation:

_____
_____
_____
_____

Thoughts about today:

_____
_____
_____
_____
_____
_____
_____
_____

My Mood Today

1   2   3   4   5   6   7   8   9   10

I stayed sober today: ◯ YES   ◯ NO

Resources

Emergency Services

Dial "9-1-1"

SAMHSA's National Helpline
1-800-662-HELP

Confidential, free, 24-hour-a-day, 365-day-a-year, information service, in English and Spanish, for individuals and family members facing mental and/or substance use disorders.

The National Suicide Prevention Lifeline
1-800-273-TALK

Suicide prevention, drug and alcohol abuse

"For I know the plans I have for you,"
declares the Lord,
"plans to prosper you and not to harm you,
plans to give you **HOPE** *and a* **FUTURE."**

JEREMIAH 29:11

Made in the USA
San Bernardino, CA
17 March 2019